GREEK MYTHOLOGY

THE AGONY OF ATLAS

Graphic Planet
An Imprint of Magic Wagon
abdobooks.com

THIS BOOK IS DEDICATED TO MY SCHOOLTEACHERS THROUGHOUT THE YEARS. TEACHING SO MANY KIDS, PREPARING US FOR THE LIVES THAT LAY AHEAD, WAS TRULY AS IF THE WEIGHT OF OUR FUTURE WORLD WAS ON YOUR SHOULDERS—BECAUSE IT WAS. -DC

TO EVERYONE WHO LOVES A GREAT GREEK STORY ESPECIALLY MY CAT MIMITO. ILLUSTRATING THIS COLLECTION WAS CHALLENGING AND FUN. I LOVED THE WHOLE PROCESS. -LA

abdobooks.com

Published by Magic Wagon, a division of ABDO, PO Box 398166, Minneapolis, Minnesota 55439.
Copyright © 2022 by Abdo Consulting Group, Inc. International copyrights reserved in all countries.
No part of this book may be reproduced in any form without written permission from the publisher.
Graphic Planet™ is a trademark and logo of Magic Wagon.

Printed in the United States of America, North Mankato, Minnesota.
102021
012022

THIS BOOK CONTAINS
RECYCLED MATERIALS

Written by David Campiti
Illustrated and Colored by Lelo Alves
Lettered by Kathryn S. Renta
Editorial Supervision by David Campiti/MJ Macedo
Packaged by Glass House Graphics
Research Assistance by Matt Simmons
Art Directed by Candice Keimig
Editorial Support by Tamara L. Britton

Library of Congress Control Number: 2021941220

Publisher's Cataloging-in-Publication Data

Names: Campiti, David, author. | Alves, Lelo, illustrator.
Title: The agony of Atlas / by David Campiti ; illustrated by Lelo Alves.
Description: Minneapolis, Minnesota : Magic Wagon, 2022. | Series: Greek mythology
Summary: Atlas bears the weight of the world on his shoulders in a graphic novel interpretation of this classic Greek myth.
Identifiers: ISBN 9781098231798 (lib. bdg.) | ISBN 9781644946619 (pbk.) | ISBN 9781098232351 (ebook) | ISBN 9781098232634 (Read-to-Me ebook)
Subjects: LCSH: Titans (Mythology)--Juvenile fiction. | Mythology, Greek--Juvenile fiction. | Gods, Greek--Juvenile fiction. | Heroes--Juvenile fiction. | Adventure stories--Juvenile fiction. | Graphic Novels--Juvenile fiction.
Classification: DDC 741.5--dc23

TABLE OF CONTENTS

CHARACTER
GUIDE 4

THE AGONY OF
ATLAS 5

WHAT DO
YOU THINK? 30

MYSTERIES
BEHIND THE MYTHS 31

GLOSSARY &
ONLINE RESOURCES 32

CHARACTER GUIDE

ATLAS
ENDURING TITAN

HERMES
TRICKSTER & FLEET MESSENGER

URANUS
EMBODIMENT OF THE HEAVENS

GAIA
ANCESTRAL EARTH MOTHER

ZEUS
KING OF THE GODS

HERA
GODDESS OF WOMEN

CRONUS
TITAN RULER

HYPERION
TITAN SON OF URANUS AND GAIA

PROMETHEUS
THINKING MAN'S TITAN

PYTHIA
ORACLE AT DELPHI

HERACLES
SON OF ZEUS

PERSEUS
SON OF ZEUS

AS CRONUS'S LOYAL FOLLOWER, ATLAS LED HIS BROTHERS INTO FIERCE BATTLE WITH THE GREAT GOD ZEUS --

-- A WAR THAT RAGED WITH UNWAVERING FURY FOR TEN LONG YEARS.

TITANS AGAINST GODS, GIANTS OVER THEM ALL --

-- EVEN AS ATLAS'S OWN BROTHERS PROMETHEUS AND EPIMETHEUS SIDED WITH ZEUS RATHER THAN WITH THEIR OWN FATHER...

...AGAINST WHOM THEY FOUGHT FOR SUPREMACY OF THE COSMOS.

KAROOOM!

YES. YES, PERHAPS THAT WILL DO.

ATLAS DOES NOT TAKE HERA'S TASK LIGHTLY.

DESIRING TO KNOW WHAT LAY AHEAD, HE JOURNEYS UNDER COVER OF NIGHT --

-- TO THE CITY OF DELPHI --

SPEAK TRUTH, DEAR ORACLE.

WHAT FATE AWAITS THE GOLDEN APPLES MY KINGDOM PROTECTS FOR GODDESS HERA?

-- TO MEET WITH THE ORACLE, PYTHIA.

SHE BREATHES IN NOXIOUS FUMES FROM A DECAYING DRAGON KILLED BY APOLLO ON THIS VERY SPOT --

-- AND IT IMBUES HER WITH PRECIOUS POWER THAT UNFOLDS THE FUTURE.

I SEE HERA'S FEARS WELL-FOUNDED.

A CHILD OF ZEUS TAKES THE APPLES FROM YOUR LANDS AND CAUSES YOUR UNDOING.

PYTHIA'S WORDS ARE CLIPPED AND CLEAR, NO MISINTERPRETATION POSSIBLE.

20

ATLAS RUSHES HOME, FULL OF FEAR, ONLY TO DISCOVER HIS MANY DAUGHTERS -- TRAPPED!

FATHER!

SAVE US!

WHAT HAS HAPPENED HERE??

YOU'VE KEPT BUSY SINCE ESCAPING TARTARUS, TITAN!

BUT MY SCHEMING WIFE COULDN'T HIDE YOU FROM MY SIGHTS FOREVER!

ZEUS!!

YOU'VE SIRED MANY OFFSPRING AND COMMANDED QUITE A KINGDOM.

NOW LET THE COSMOS CRUSH THEM TO DUST!

NO!

ESCAPE, MY CHILDREN! I WILL KEEP THE SKIES AT BAY!

HAHAHA! INDEED YOU WILL!

IIIEEE!

EH -- ?

SNAPPP!

SURELY, FATHER, YOU MUST CONSIDER REMAINING FREE!

AND SO HE DOES!

HERACLES, GIVEN THE IMPORTANCE OF THESE APPLES TO HERA AND MY PROMISE TO HER --

-- I THINK IT WISE THAT I DELIVER THEM TO YOUR KING EURYSTHEUS MYSELF. SO WE MAY LIAISE A KING-TO-KING UNDERSTANDING.

...YOURSELF?

IT IS...WISE THAT YOU FORGE AN UNDERSTANDING WITH A FELLOW KING, ATLAS!

I WILL CONTINUE TO HOLD THE SKY FOR YOU, IN THE MEANTIME.

I ONLY ASK THAT YOU TAKE THE SKY -- FOR BUT A MOMENT -- SO THAT I MAY FIND CUSHIONING FOR MY SHOULDERS.

FOR IT IS A GREAT WEIGHT, AND I AM NOT A TITAN NOR AS POWERFUL AS YOU.

BUT OF COURSE -- !

25

26

AS YEARS WENT BY, ATLAS'S SUBJECTS NO LONGER ADDRESSED HIM. HE GREW OLDER, MORE WEARY, MORE AFRAID HE WOULD NEVER BE FREED.

ATLAS CLUNG TO HOPE THAT HERA WOULD FREE HIM BECAUSE HE AND HIS DAUGHTERS NEVER CEASED CARING FOR HER TREE.

BUT WE GODS ARE FICKLE, AND ATLAS IN HIS AGONY HAD BECOME BITTER AND LESS THAN RATIONAL.

STILL HE KNEW THAT, WITHOUT HIM, THE HEAVENS AND THE EARTH WOULD CRASH INTO ONE ANOTHER.

SO HE WAS NOT PREPARED TO WELCOME A VISITOR!

HISSSS
HISSSS
HISSSS
SSSSS SSSS
DRIP DRIP
SNAPP

ATLAS! I HAVE LONG HEARD OF YOUR STRUGGLE, DEAR TITAN!

I AM PERSEUS, SON OF ZEUS. I HAVE TRAVELED LONG AND HARD, AND I AM BEYOND SPENT.

..."PERSEUS"?

MAY I ENJOY THE HOSPITALITY OF YOUR KINGDOM?

MIGHT I RECEIVE SOME DRINK, BREAKFAST, AND BED TO RESTORE MY WEARY BONES?

PERSEUS -- SON OF ZEUS? YOUR FATHER DID THIS TO ME!

LONG HAS IT BEEN PROPHESIZED THAT A SON OF ZEUS WOULD COME TO STEAL HERA'S GOLDEN APPLES.

SO I CANNOT -- I WILL NOT -- GRANT YOU HOSPITALITY OR ACCESS TO MY KINGDOM!

PAIN AND EXHAUSTION CAN MUDDLE THE MINDS OF THE BEST OF MEN, OR GODS, OR TITANS.

27

WHAT DO YOU THINK?

1. Upon hearing that Perseus is a son of Zeus, Atlas immediately denies him hospitality of any kind and demands that he leave, fearing the prophesy that a son of Zeus would steal Hera's golden apples. Was Atlas right to deny food or drink or lodging to Perseus? Why or why not? What should he have done?

2. Atlas and Perseus meet as two heroes connecting at the worst possible moment. Perseus has just completed a journey of perilous adventures and is exhausted. Atlas was doomed to hold up the heavens and is in great pain. Had they met under different circumstances, how might each have reacted and behaved?

3. Greek legend has it that, while Atlas held up the heavens, he shifted his body occasionally, which accounted for the movements of the stars in the heavens. This gave a means of navigation for sailors and a way for farmers to distinguish between the seasons, making him quite a useful god to the Greeks. What other characteristics might Atlas be known for?

4. Zeus's punishment of Atlas was also a way to punish Gaia and Uranus to prevent them from ever coming together again. What all might have happened if Atlas were unable to continue holding up the sky?

5. There are multiple stories about Atlas. One tells of Atlas as a mere shepherd when Perseus turned him to stone. Another describes Atlas as the first king of Atlantis. There is yet another that makes him king of the land of Mauri in Africa. What was the first Atlas story you ever heard or read?

MYSTERIES BEHIND THE MYTHS

1. Images of Atlas holding up a world are not traditionally meant to be holding up Earth but, rather, a celestial sphere. This imagined Earth to be in its center at a fixed point, and the stars to be projected outward from it, for purposes of studying.

2. Building on the idea of Atlas and the world, and his interest in map making or cartography, an Atlas is a collection of maps. Atlases were so named by cartographer Gerardus Mercator. Aside from geographical information, they may contain information about economic, religious, or political boundaries. Atlases were traditionally books but today are found in many formats.

3. Some versions of an Atlas legend, such as one penned by the Athenian philosopher Plato, cast Atlas as the first king of Atlantis. In this telling, his father was Poseidon and his mother was a mortal woman, Cleito. In other versions of this story, his mother was Gaia and his father was Uranus. Those versions do not directly connect to the Atlas who held the heavens.

4. For his eleventh labor, in some versions of the myths Heracles never looked back after Atlas brought him the golden apples and once again shouldered the heavens. In others, much as he saved Prometheus, Heracles later returned to build two pillars to hold up the heavens, rescuing Atlas from his eternal burden.

5. The Rock of Gibraltar on the Iberian peninsula between Spain and Portugal is considered to be one of the pillars Heracles built. The other is Jebel Musa in Morocco, Africa. From the Rock of Gibraltar, you can see Africa and the Jebel Musa mountain across the water. The Garden of the Hesperides is at the base of the Atlas Mountains in Africa.

GLOSSARY

ATLAS — Known for his endurance and strength, Atlas was the son of the Titan Iapetus and the Oceanid Clymene, brother of Epirthemius and Prometheus. He was also known as a king who studied the stars and, as such, invented astronomy. After the Titanomachy, Zeus doomed Atlas to hold up the heavens, forever separating Gaia (earth) from Uranus (sky).

CHAOS — The vast void at the dawn of time, which gave form to Erebus (darkness), Eros (desire), Gaia (earth), Tartarus (the abyss), and Nyx (night), the foundations of the universe.

CRONUS — Direct descendant of Gaia (earth) and Uranus (sky), ruler and youngest of the first generation of Titans. He and the goddess Rhea were parents of Chiron, Demeter, Hades, Hera, Hestia, and Zeus.

GAIA — The personification of earth, considered the ancestral mother of all life. From her came the Cyclopes, the Giants, and the Titans.

GREECE — A mountainous country with many islands, located on the Mediterranean Sea. Considered the birthplace of democracy and early mathematical and scientific principles and the place from which the gods ruled.

HERACLES — Mortal son of Zeus and the human Alcmene, whom Zeus' wife Hera tried to have killed on multiple occasions. Among his many accomplishments were completing twelve labors, the "impossible tasks" put upon him by King Eurystheus

HERMES — The divine trickster, son of Zeus and Maia, the emissary and fleet messenger of the gods. He even conducted souls into the afterlife.

MOUNT OLYMPUS — A real mountain in Thessaly, Greece, towering nearly 9,800 feet (2,987 m) above the sea. This is the site around which the mythology for the gods was created.

OLYMPIA — The fabled city that the gods inhabited and from which Zeus ruled, located at the top of Mount Olympus.

PROMETHEUS — A Titan with intelligence and forethought, usually considering the consequences an action or decision might bring. He tricked and stole from Zeus to champion mankind, and in so doing suffered Zeus's wrath.

TITANS — The twelve children of first-ever parents Gaia and Uranus. Their loyalties split in the great war, the Titanomachy, in which Zeus overthrew his father Cronus for supremacy.

TITANOMACHY — The ten-year war fought among the Titans and the Olympians, as Zeus battled his father Cronus for control of the cosmos. Zeus's Olympians were victorious.

ZEUS — God of lightning, son of Cronus and Rhea, husband to Hera, he fought a great and terrible war to become king of the gods of Olympus.

Booklinks
NONFICTION NETWORK
FREE! ONLINE NONFICTION RESOURCES

To learn more about **GREEK MYTHOLOGY**, visit *abdobooklinks.com* or scan this QR code. These links are routinely monitored and updated to provide the most current information available.